My Vote Counts!

**First-time voters tell about
their election experiences.**

★★★★★★★★★★★★★★★★★★★★★★★★★★★★★

by Siniria Paulino, Juda Mann, Luciana Nikolajevic,
Marvin Mathew, and Violet Zektser

★★★★★★★★★★★ **Table of Contents** ★★★★★★★★★★★

Voting

You Decide Who Makes the Important Decisions

More than 400 years ago, a group of settlers came from England to the New World. The newcomers established the colony of Jamestown, Virginia. One of the first things they did was hold an **election**. They voted for the president of the new settlement.

Elections go back even farther than that. The ancient Greeks held elections 2,500 years ago! Throughout most of history, the right to vote to elect leaders has been a privilege. Wars have been fought to get—or to keep—the right to elect leaders by voting.

Jamestown, Virginia

ancient Greece

The United States of America is a **democracy**. The word "democracy" comes from Greek words that mean "the rule of the people." In a democracy, people vote to choose their leaders. And by choosing their leaders, the people have a say in how their government is run. All U.S. **citizens** eighteen years and older have the right to vote. They vote on Election Day in November.

In the United States, people vote by a secret **ballot**. Whom you vote for is your choice, and it's your business.

president   senator   representative   governor

Voting is important because the people who are elected run the government. These elected officials or officeholders make many decisions that affect our lives. They make laws about how much in taxes people pay. They decide how much money goes to education, and how much goes to protect the environment. They also decide if the country should go to war, and how much to spend on the military. It's the responsibility of all good citizens to express their opinions by voting in elections.

You can't start voting until you turn eighteen. But you're never too old to vote. In 2012 Joanna Jenkins, an African American woman who lives in South Carolina, voted for the first time. She was 108! Because the elderly Ms. Jenkins had trouble speaking, her cousin Shirley Lee described the situation to a newspaper reporter.

"We were looking at the presidential debates on TV, and, all of a sudden, Joanna decided she wanted to vote," Shirley explained. "She was excited to vote."

However, Ms. Jenkins thought she would not be allowed to vote. She could not read or write. She did not have a state identification card. But she got some help from the people who run the elections. So in 2012, for the first time in her life, Joanna Jenkins exercised her precious right to vote.

After voting, Ms. Jenkins expressed her pride in her accomplishment with the simple words: "I feel good!"

In the coming pages, see how other first-time voters feel about voting. Read what they have to say about the responsibility and the satisfaction they got from exercising their right to vote.

Joanna Jenkins, age 108, voted for the first time in 2012.

Being Part of History

Siniria Paulino, 18, is a student at SUNY Rockland Community College. She is secretary of the student government executive board. She is a member of Future Business Leaders of America. Her parents are from the Dominican Republic.

November 6, 2012, was the first time I ever voted. For me, voting is something I always knew I would do. As a first-generation American, it is an extreme honor for me and my family to have the **liberty** to vote.

My parents came to this country at a very young age. They only recently became American citizens. In 2010 my mother was **sworn in** as an American. She cried with joy. She told me that it was the biggest honor one could hope for as an **immigrant**. She also voted for the first time in 2012. Now her voice matters in the country she has considered her home for many years.

To me, voting was much more than getting up early and going to the **polls** to fill in some circles on paper ballots. Voting gave me the power on Election Day. My opinion on who should govern and enforce the laws mattered. In this country, unlike some others in the world, my voice counts!

Voting on Election Day was an experience I will always remember. I felt important. The polling place had such a good feeling, too. The workers were so polite and helpful. You could tell that they, too, were happy to be there.

One thing surprised me, though. The volunteers seemed amazed to see someone as young as me coming out to vote. They told me that many young people don't vote. I came out of the voting place feeling more important than ever. I knew that, no matter who won the election, my voice was heard. I was part of history.

7

It's Our Future

Juda Mann is a 19-year-old college student who plans to make a career in architecture. Juda has had a number of part-time jobs, including lifeguarding, waiting on tables, babysitting, and working for a moving service.

What got me interested in politics was my curiosity about how politics and government work. I have a friend who wants to go into politics. We often have conversations about political **candidates** and what they stand for. We also talk about laws that are being passed.

To be honest, my first voting experience, in 2012, was not what I expected. I thought there would be armed guards there to make sure nobody did anything suspicious. But I was glad to see that it wasn't like that. Everything there was calm. The election workers were happy to have people show up. They congratulated all of the first-time voters, like me. The good wishes from so many strangers made me feel special, like a kid at his birthday party.

I was nervous voting for the first time. I felt like I was taking my college entrance exams all over again. When it came time to cast my ballot, I made sure that I read all the voting instructions. And I checked to make sure that I filled in the voting circles on the ballot completely.

sample ballots

After I filled in the ballot, I relaxed. Now all I had to do was wait on line to feed my ballot into the scanning/counting machine. An election worker who was sitting nearby thanked and congratulated me again for voting.

When it was over, I thought about some of the problems our country is having. Voting, to me, meant that I finally could have a say in our future. After all, it is my—I mean *our*—future we're dealing with.

Power to Choose

Luciana Nikolajevic, 34, came to the United States from Brazil seven years ago. She is a dental assistant and is making plans to enroll in a dental hygiene program. Luciana feels that completing dental hygiene school will lead to greater career opportunities.

When I came to the United States from Brazil, I spoke very little English. I studied hard, and just last year I passed the test to become an American citizen. Finally, I would be able to vote! When I lived in Brazil, I had already voted a few times. So it was upsetting for me that I could not vote in the United States—until now. After I voted here for the first time in 2012, I felt like a full, true American. And, later that day, I felt even better because my candidates won.

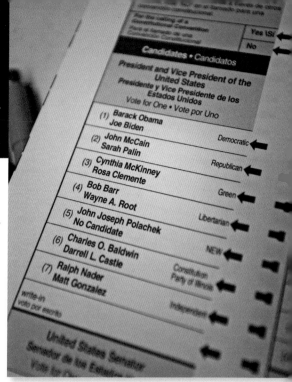

I had a wonderful experience on Election Day. I was proud for making my vote count in helping to decide the future of our nation. It was a little complicated to understand the voting sheet. But after taking my time to read the instructions, I was able to vote for the people I wanted.

I love living in a democracy. The right to vote makes me feel that I'm part of the society I live in. Voting gives me the power to help choose who is going to **represent** my concerns. By voting, I help pick the people who will fight to improve my country and the lives of all of us.

Democracy Is a Beautiful Thing

Marvin Mathew, 21, is a student at the University of Maryland. He majors in government and politics. He is active in student groups and political organizations. Marvin's family is from India, but he was born in the United States.

When I voted for the first time in 2012, I couldn't stop smiling. Voting, for me, is the opportunity that our American forefathers created so that our voices and opinions could be heard. By voting I can help decide the course of our nation. I can help choose the people I believe will provide effective leadership. Democracy is a beautiful thing. Many people in the Middle East and Africa, for example, are fighting to get the freedoms and rights we have had in America for over 200 years.

"Proud" and "blessed" are two words to describe my first experience in voting. But as good as it felt to vote, I realize that too many Americans do not vote. That's a little saddening. It inspires me to work to create and support programs to encourage people to first get **registered** to vote. I work with government programs and student organizations to make it easier for people to register and vote.

I also strive to help get young people involved in government affairs. I'm dedicated to encouraging the participation of young people in politics and government. I want to help them to become the leaders of the future.

Young people are innovative and creative. It's time for us to take our great ideas and make them happen. With good training and the right leadership, young people are more than capable. It is our responsibility to build a brighter future for the world, while protecting the rights of all.

Campaign workers celebrate their candidate's victory on Election Day.

Maybe One Day You Will Be Voting for Marvin!

★ ★ Marvin is not only very interested and involved in American government, he also has his eye on world affairs. He represented the United States at the One Young World conference in 2012 in Pittsburgh, Pennsylvania, and participated in the Clinton Global Initiative University in 2010. He has also attended the Naval Academy Foreign Affairs Conference. These events gave him the opportunity to meet former president Bill Clinton and former United Nations secretary general Kofi Annan. ★

Volunteer

****

Violet Zektser, 20, was born in Russia. At age 5 she came to the United States with her family. Violet grew up in Brooklyn, New York. She plans to study social work at Hunter College in Manhattan. Her voting experience shows that local elections are important, too.

I was a first-time voter in 2012. It was fascinating! Everyone was so secretive. When I first entered the voting place, I was given a ballot and sent to a private booth to fill out my voting ballot in secret. I was told not to show my ballot to anyone. I didn't think it was a big deal if others knew whom I was voting for.

To me, my first-time election experience meant a lot more than voting. I saw the election process close up. I worked on the **campaign** to reelect my state senator, David Storobin.

Senator Storobin had been the first Russian–Jewish immigrant to run for state senator in New York. I got involved in politics through someone whom I met a couple of years ago in an organization called RAJE (the Russian American Jewish Experience). The elections were important to me because I felt that my community in Brooklyn needed to keep Storobin as senator. He wanted to do so much, like creating more jobs, keeping taxes low, and supporting education.

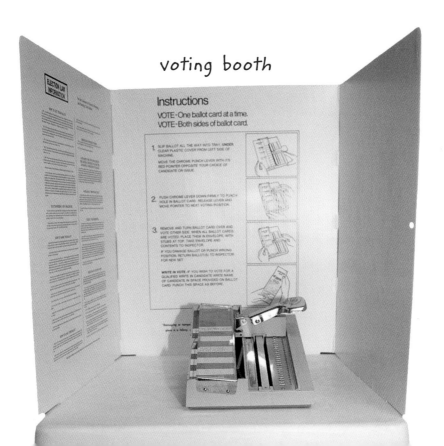

voting booth

I started out as a campaign volunteer at the end of September. After a couple of weeks, I got promoted to campaign worker. One of my jobs was handing out flyers. On Election Day, I stood on a street corner near the polling place from 7 A.M. until 9 P.M. distributing flyers for Senator Storobin. Not only was it cold that day, but it was hard work. Most people were nice, but one guy ripped up a flyer right in front of my face. I guess that was his way of saying he wasn't going to vote for my candidate.

Sadly, Senator Storobin was not reelected, and my job ended. But I was glad that I voted for him. Even though he lost, I learned a lot about elections. I enjoyed working in the campaign, too, and I met some great people. It felt really good to do the right thing—voting and supporting my candidate.

ELECT

SENATOR DAVID

STOROBIN

STOROBIN FOR SENATOR

Make Your Voice Heard

Voting is not the only way you can help pick your leaders. If you strongly believe in your candidate, you can volunteer to help a candidate's election campaign. As a volunteer, you can:

- make phone calls to encourage other voters to vote for your candidate

- stuff envelopes with letters to voters asking for their vote

- put up posters for your candidate

- stand outdoors handing out flyers promoting your candidate

- organize parties and other events to raise money for the campaign.

Election campaigns usually use both volunteers and paid campaign workers. Political candidates always need help. Maybe one day you'll volunteer to help elect a person you strongly believe in.

Glossary

ballot   (BA-lut) *noun* a ticket or piece of paper used to vote in an election (page 3)

campaign   (kam-PANE) *noun* a set of activities coordinated by supporters of a political candidate to win over voters (page 18)

candidates   (KAN-dih-datez) *noun* people who officially run for election to a government position (page 8)

citizens   (SIH-tih-zenz) *noun* people who have full rights in a country either because they were born there or because they have gone through the official process of citizenship (page 3)

democracy   (dih-MAH-kruh-see) *noun* a form of government in which people choose their leaders by voting (page 3)

election   (ih-LEK-shun) *noun* a scheduled event in which voters choose a candidate to fill a political office (page 2)

immigrant   (IH-mih-grunt) *noun* a person who comes to a country to live there (page 6)

liberty   (LIH-ber-tee) *noun* the power to choose what you want, such as to vote in an election (page 6)

polls   (POLEZ) *noun* places set up for people to vote on Election Day (page 7)

registered   (REH-jih-sterd) *verb* enrolled on an official voters list, as required by law (page 15)

represent   (reh-prih-ZENT) *verb* to perform the duties of your government position through speaking and taking action to benefit many people (page 13)

sworn in   (SWORN IN) *verb* given the rights of a citizen after promising out loud to be honest and loyal to your new country (page 6)

Analyze the Text

Questions for Close Reading

Use facts and details from the text to support your answers to the following questions.

- In the last paragraph of her narrative on page 7, Siniria Paulino says she was surprised that the volunteers "seemed amazed to see someone as young as me coming out to vote." Why do you think this surprised Siniria? How did this make her feel? Base your answers on the text only.

- Marvin Mathew is active in student government and political organizations. Cite evidence in the text to support this statement. What specific comment does Marvin make that explains why he is so active?

- The Introduction states that Joanna Jenkins exercised her "precious" right to vote for the first time at age 108. Why was the word *precious* chosen?

Comprehension: Compare and Contrast

The five people in this book all voted for the first time as American citizens in the 2012 election. Who was born in the U.S.? Who was born elsewhere? How did this impact their voting experience?

Person	Born in U.S.	Not Born in U.S.	Impact on Voting
Siniria Paulino			
Juda Mann			
Luciana Nikolajevic			
Marvin Mathew			
Violet Zektser			